AF598975

It's as Clear as a Bell!

by Cynthia Amoroso ✶ illustrated by Mernie Gallagher-Cole

Wonder Books
An Imprint of The Child's World®
childsworld.com

Published by The Child's World®
800-599-READ • childsworld.com

ISBN Information
9781503865624 (Reinforced Library Binding)
9781503866119 (Portable Document Format)
9781503866959 (Online Multi-user eBook)
9781503867796 (Electronic Publication)

LCCN 2022939523

Printed in the United States of America

ABOUT THE AUTHOR

As a daughter of elementary and English teachers, Cynthia Amoroso grew up in a home that was filled with language. She spent many hours enjoying reading and writing. Later, she followed in the footsteps of both her parents and became a teacher. As a high school English teacher and as an elementary teacher, Cynthia shared her love of language with students. She has always been fascinated with idioms and other figures of speech as they reflect and represent the culture and people who use them.

ABOUT THE ILLUSTRATOR

Mernie Gallagher-Cole lives in Pennsylvania with her husband and children. She uses idioms like the ones in this book every day. She has illustrated many children's books as well as greeting cards, puzzles, and games.

Contents

People use **idioms** every day. These are sayings and phrases with meanings that are different from the actual words. Some idioms seem silly. Many of them don't make much sense . . . at first.

This book will help you understand some of the most common idioms. The illustrations will show you how you might hear a saying or phrase. And the accompanying examples and definitions will tell you how the idiom is used, what it really means, and where it **originated**. All of these idioms—even the silly or humorous ones—are a rich, colorful part of the English language. You'll soon see that understanding idioms and knowing how to use them is a piece of cake!

All that glitters is not gold

Nine-year-old Madison was excited. "Jude just got a job at a movie theater," she said. "I'd like to work there, too. I love watching movies!"

"Do you know what Jude does?" asked Mom.

"Not exactly," said Madison.

"He sells tickets, and then he cleans up after the show," she replied. "Jude doesn't get to watch the movies. Working in a theater might seem like your dream job. But remember—all that glitters is not gold!"

MEANING: *Things aren't always as nice as they seem; appearances can be* ***deceiving***

ORIGIN: *This popular saying has been around since the 1400s. It has appeared in many variations and in several languages! This idiom was first used in the United States in the mid-1800s. Miners looking for gold in the West were sometimes tricked by spotting something they thought was gold. However, it was actually a yellowish, sparkly mineral called iron pyrite—known as fool's gold—and was not worth any money.*

As happy as a clam

John was excited to spend the afternoon with his two-year-old cousin, Nathan. John wanted to show him lots of things! After his aunt dropped him off, Nathan was cranky and didn't want to play. John tried to cheer him up, but finally gave up and went outside. When he came back in, he asked his mom if Nathan was in a better mood.

"He sure is," said John's mom. "I let him play with some of your old cars. He loves them! Look at him now—he's as happy as a clam."

MEANING: *Enjoying what you are doing; in a good mood; happy and content*

ORIGIN: *The full* ***expression*** *is "as happy as a clam at high tide." It was created by fishermen and marine workers in the early 1800s to describe all the clams they'd spot during high tide. At that time of day, there were fewer sea birds and other animals by the water. So the clams were in less danger of being eaten, and they could swim and move around freely.*

Beauty is in the eye of the beholder

Caitlin was standing in the doorway of her little sister's bedroom.

"Mom," she asked, "is that really the color Meg picked out?"

Her mom nodded. "It's quite bright, isn't it?" she said.

"It sure is," Caitlin replied. "I couldn't stand having my room painted that color!"

"I know," said Mom. "But Meg absolutely loves it. Just remember—beauty is in the eye of the beholder!"

MEANING: *What is beautiful to one person might not look as good to someone else*

ORIGIN: *Beauty is* ***subjective****, meaning that different people have different ideas about what is beautiful. This popular saying dates back hundreds of years. Many famous people, such as Benjamin Franklin and William Shakespeare, have used variations of it. Many people believe the writer Margaret Wolfe Hungerford created this particular wording of the phrase in 1878.*

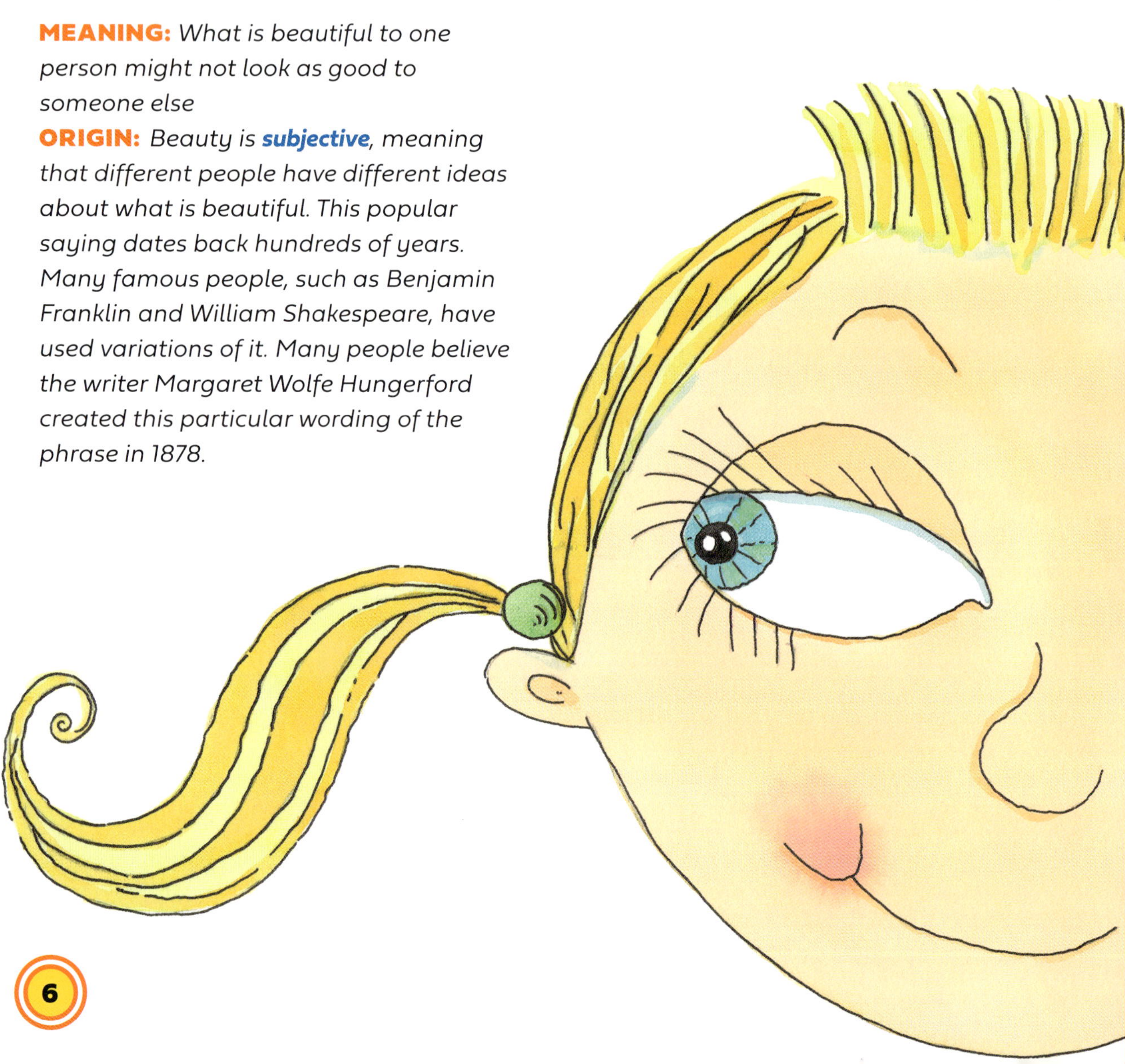

Bite your tongue

Anna had just come from softball practice. "How did it go?" asked her dad.

"It was really frustrating," said Anna. "Molly kept complaining again. She only joined the team a month ago, but she thinks she knows everything! Mom said to just ignore her, but it's hard. When Molly started complaining about Kayla's pitching, I really had to bite my tongue!"

MEANING: *To keep yourself from saying something you might regret; to take back or feel bad about something you just said*

ORIGIN: *If you bite down on your tongue and hold it between your teeth, it is almost impossible to speak. So biting your tongue is a way to stop yourself from saying something you might regret. Some people credit this saying to William Shakespeare. The expression has been in use for hundreds of years.*

A bull in a china shop

Noah's family had a gigantic dog named Ace. Noah was really excited—Ace had just passed his test to be a therapy dog! Now he would be able to visit people who were sick or feeling sad.

"Where are we going to take him?" Noah asked his mom. "Can he go to that nursing home where Grandma used to live? They'd love him there!"

"They sure would," agreed Mom. "But Ace is kind of big and clumsy for a place like that. He'd be like a bull in a china shop!"

MEANING: *Something that is out of place, or clumsy in a situation that calls for great care*

ORIGIN: *This saying is based on a* ***fable*** *by Aesop. The original story is about a donkey in a potter's shop. Over time, the story changed, but the meaning remained the same. "China" refers to expensive, finely made dishes. This saying is also used to describe someone who says or does something that is careless or upsets others.*

Can't see the forest for the trees

"How does Sophie like her new internship?" asked Ryan.

"She's not sure yet," Ryan's mom replied. "Your cousin is feeling a little frustrated because there's so much to learn."

"Right now, Sophie can't see the forest for the trees," explained Dad. "She's so busy trying to learn all the little parts of her job that she can't even think about what it all means."

MEANING: *To pay so much attention to details that you don't see the big picture; to focus on small details and not understand the whole situation*

ORIGIN: *This saying first appeared in the mid-1500s in a book of* ***proverbs****. The original expression was "Ye cannot see the wood for the trees." The meaning has always referred to paying too much attention to the details and missing the bigger picture.*

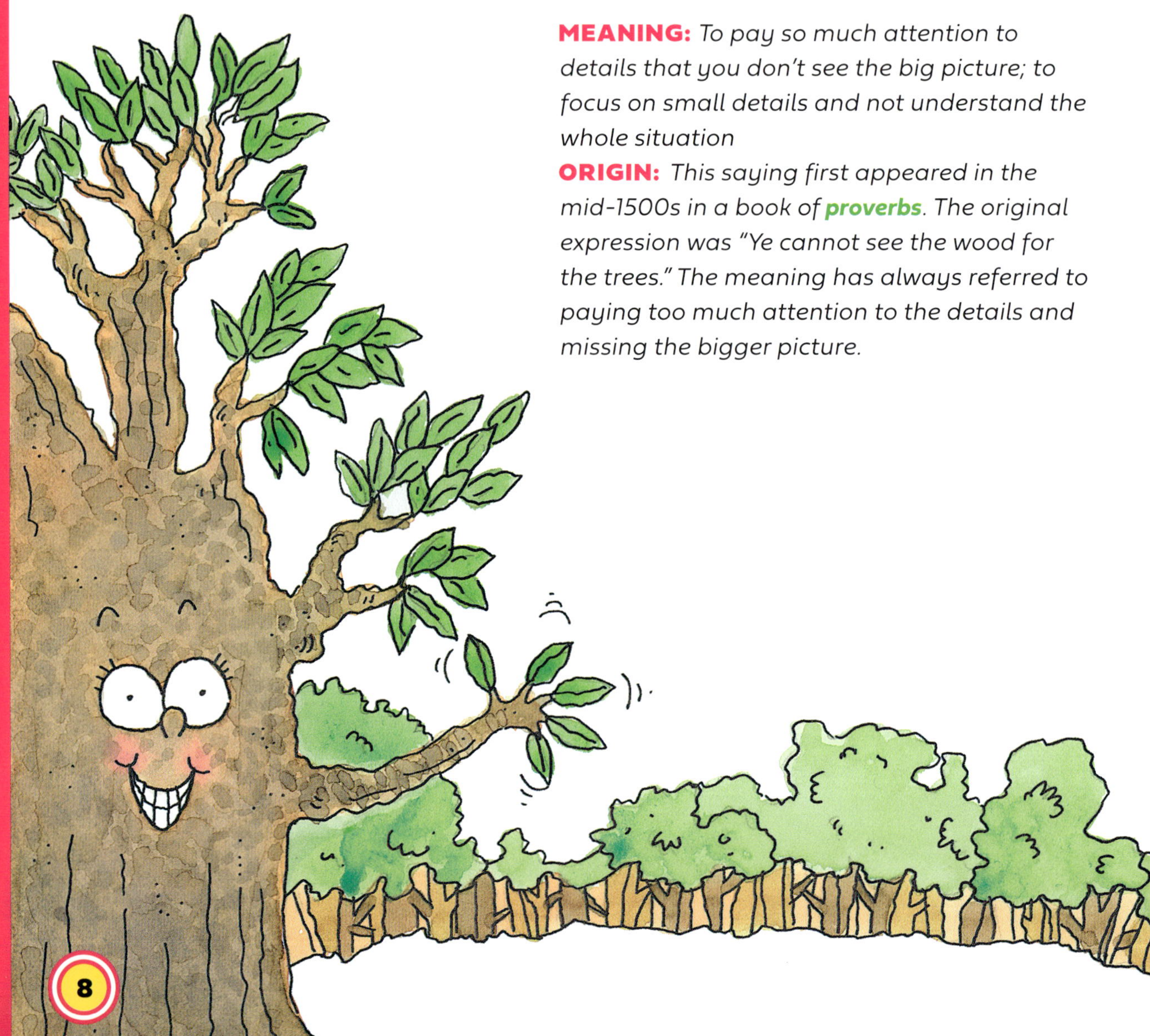

Clear as a bell

Simon and his brother were having a water fight when their dad came outside to find them.

"OK, guys," said Dad to the two boys, "you need to put the hose down for a while. I'd like to get these rose bushes planted before your mom gets home. She'll really be happy! But we're going to have to work fast. No more playing around until we're done! Is that clear?"

"Clear as a bell!" said Simon. He grinned at his brother. "We can settle this later."

MEANING: *Clearly and easily understood*

ORIGIN: *Bells have been rung through the ages for many different reasons: to gather people together, to warn people, to remind people of something, among other uses. Bells are loud and have a clear sound so they can be heard across long distances. This saying is a* ***simile****, referring to something that is understood easily without any confusion.*

Cute as a bug's ear

Aunt Emily heard voices through her front door. "Trick or treat!" the voices said.

When Aunt Emily opened the door, Jake and his whole family cried, "Happy Halloween!" All of the kids were wearing costumes.

"Oh my!" said Aunt Emily, smiling. "I see a ghost, and a witch, and . . . well, will you look at that? It's little Amy, dressed up as a pumpkin! She's as cute as a bug's ear!"

MEANING: *Very cute*

ORIGIN: *Most people agree that this simile dates back to the 1800s. Its exact origin is unknown. This expression is mostly used in the United States as a humorous way to describe something that is adorable.*

Double whammy

Uncle Peter called his nephew Eric on the phone. "Hey, buddy," he said when Eric answered, "your dad told me about your skateboard accident. How are you feeling?"

"Terrible," replied Eric. "First I break my ankle, and then I catch this stupid cold. All I can do is sit on the couch. I'm really bored!"

"A broken ankle and a cold? Ugh!" said Uncle Peter. "You poor guy, that's really a double whammy! Why don't I bring over a movie and keep you company for a while?"

MEANING: *Two bad things happening at the same time*

ORIGIN: *Most people agree this phrase first referred to an evil spell or something related to witchcraft. Later it was used to describe two negative things happening at the same time or back-to-back.*

Ducks in a row

Corey's big sister, Kristin, had been in her room all day, with the door shut.

"What's she up to?" Corey asked their mom. "That seems really weird."

"Well, remember," said Mom, "Kristin's got that college interview on Friday. She really wants to make a good impression, so she's spending a lot of time getting everything ready. She needs to have all her ducks in a row."

MEANING: *To have everything in order ahead of time*

ORIGIN: *Some people believe this expression comes from a lawn game that was popular in the 1700s. Others believe that the phrase* ***alludes*** *to ducks lined up in flight, or the way ducklings line up and follow their mother.*

Fresh as a daisy

Kelly came back from the park early.

"Did you have fun?" Kelly's mom asked.

"Nope," Kelly replied. "It's too hot out! But Dawn had a great time."

"Dawn is just like her mother," said Kelly's mom with a laugh. "The heat doesn't bother her, and she never seems tired. Everyone else can be exhausted and dripping wet, but she's always fresh as a daisy!"

MEANING: *Well rested; full of energy; bright and cheerful*

ORIGIN: *This saying refers to a daisy opening its petals in the morning sun. It was often used in literature dating back to the late 1300s.*

Handwriting on the wall

Zach and his friends were worried. They heard that the city was thinking about redoing Century Park and replacing the skate park with pickleball courts. Zach's dad had just talked to a friend on the city council.

"Well," said Dad, "the good news is that they're going to expand the other skate park down by the river. But where Century Park is concerned, I'm afraid the rumors were the handwriting on the wall. They're going to tear down that skate park next week."

MEANING: *A warning sign that something bad is going to happen*

ORIGIN: *This idiom is based on a story from the Old Testament in the Bible. In a vision, the king of Babylonia saw a mysterious message written on a wall of his palace. The writing said that his kingdom would be conquered. His kingdom was defeated shortly afterward. Today, the saying is used to describe signs that misfortune (bad luck) or trouble is coming.*

Jack-of-all-trades

"Hey, Michael, what's up?" asked Kyle when he answered the phone.

"I can't go to the lake Saturday," Michael said. "Uncle Tim's coming to town."

"Isn't he the one who bought that old house in the country?" Kyle asked.

"That's him," said Michael. "He's been fixing it up. He's been fixing up old tractors, too. He does lots of different stuff. Dad says he's a jack-of-all-trades."

MEANING: *Someone who does many different things or has skills in many areas*

ORIGIN: *A "jack" is an informal word for a laborer. This expression dates back to the 1600s and has always referred to a skilled worker who can handle a variety of tasks. The full phrase is "a jack-of-all-trades and master of none." It refers to a person who can do lots of different things but isn't an expert at any of them.*

Kick up your heels

Charlie's mom had been working overtime on a big project. Finally, she was done.

"Congratulations!" said Charlie's dad. "What are you going to do to celebrate?"

"Well," said Mom, "Roberta asked if I wanted to drive into the city this Friday to see a show, but I have a lot of catching up to do."

"Oh, go ahead!" said Dad. "You've been working really hard. Why don't you kick up your heels and have a little fun!"

MEANING: *To celebrate; to have fun*

ORIGIN: *When a horse is galloping through a field, you can see its heels kicking upward as it runs. People dancing might also lift their heels as they move around. This saying was first used around 1900 referring to a lively time or showing delight.*

Knee-jerk reaction

Patrick's dad looked tired when he came home from work.

"Did you show the proposal to your boss?" asked Mom.

"We sure did," Dad said. "He turned us down without even looking at it."

"Well, he's done that before," Mom pointed out. "It's a knee-jerk reaction whenever you show him a new idea. But after he thinks about it for a while, he usually wants to hear more."

MEANING: *To react to something without thinking; automatic*

ORIGIN: *This expression refers to the body's reflexes. If you firmly hit the spot below your knee—called the patellar reflex—your leg automatically kicks outward. This reaction is* ***spontaneous*** *and happens automatically.*

Level playing field

"How were the dance team tryouts?" Lily asked her sister, Erin.

"Better than I expected," Erin replied. "Ms. Ellis already knows some of the girls, and I was sure she had already made up her mind. But she was really nice to all of us, and she treated everybody the same. She said she'll let us know tomorrow."

"That's great!" said Lily. "You're really good, so I bet you'll make the team."

"All I wanted was a level playing field," Erin agreed. "I can do the rest."

MEANING: *A fair chance; a chance to compete under fair conditions*

ORIGIN: *This saying is a **metaphor** that refers to sports played on a field. If the playing area is on a slope, then one team will have an unfair advantage. A level, or flat, area of play provides a setting that is equal for everyone.*

Like a chicken with its head cut off

Sarah had been helping her mom all morning. They were busy getting ready for Grandma's big birthday party.

"What's next on the list, Mom?" Sarah asked.

"Well," answered Mom, "everyone will be here in an hour, and there's still a lot to do! I need a minute to think about what to do next. Otherwise, I'll just be running around like a chicken with its head cut off!"

MEANING: *Disorganized; doing things but not finishing anything*

ORIGIN: *This simile was first used around the 1800s to describe a person's disorganized or confused behavior. It's based on the fact that after a chicken is killed, its body might still move for a few moments afterward.*

Mind your own beeswax

Allison was busy on the computer, making a photo album for her parents' anniversary. She wanted it to be a surprise to everybody, and she was almost done.

Just then her brother came into the room. He wanted to use the computer, too. "What are you doing?" he asked, as Allison quickly closed the screen. "Come on, let me see!"

"Mind your own beeswax!" Allison said with a giggle. "It's a secret!"

MEANING: *To mind your own business; don't be nosy*

ORIGIN: *This expression is* **slang** *for "mind your own business." Some people believe the saying is from children's literature. It became popular around 1930. It's a humorous way to tell someone to keep out of your business.*

Out like a light

The weekend of the soccer tournament was long and hot. Trevor had played in seven games! He didn't sleep well in the hotel. After the two-hour drive home, he went straight upstairs. His dad went up to check on him later.

"How's he doing?" asked Mom when Dad came back downstairs.

Dad chuckled. "He's out like a light! He must have fallen asleep as soon as he went upstairs."

MEANING: *To fall asleep right away; unconscious*

ORIGIN: *This saying dates back to the arrival of electricity in people's homes. It dramatically changed people's way of life. This expression—which alludes to the ease of turning lights off and on with a switch—was often used to describe boxers who were knocked out during a fight.*

A penny for your thoughts

Melissa was happy. Her volleyball team had just won the championship! Best of all, she had played a great match. In her mind, she was picturing the game all over again. She was concentrating so hard, she didn't hear her dad talking to her.

"Sorry, Dad," she said, shaking her head. "I didn't even hear you."

"Is everything OK?" asked her dad. "A penny for your thoughts!"

"Everything is great, Dad," answered Melissa. "I was just thinking about my game."

MEANING: *To ask someone what they're thinking*

ORIGIN: *This idiom has appeared in literature from the 1500s. At that time, the value of a penny was much higher than it is today. The saying was a more meaningful way to tell someone that their thoughts were valuable, and you wanted to hear what they were thinking.*

Pull the plug

Jenna's family had planned to go to the water park, and they were supposed to leave soon. But Jenna was worried. Her six-year-old twin brothers kept arguing. They'd already gotten in trouble earlier, and each one kept blaming the other.

"Stop it, you guys!" Jenna said. "If you two don't behave, Mom and Dad are going to pull the plug on the whole trip!"

MEANING: *To stop something; to say no to something*

ORIGIN: *The exact origin of this expression is unknown. Some people believe it refers to removing the plug in a sink or basin to drain it. Another belief is that it's a* **euphemism** *for allowing someone to die naturally. In other words, you "pull the plug" from, or stop, the life-support machinery that is keeping a person alive.*

Raining cats and dogs

Miranda was sitting by the window, looking out at the gloomy weather.

"Phooey," she groaned. "This is terrible! We haven't been outside for three days. Is it ever going to stop raining?"

"Look at *me*!" exclaimed her brother, who had just finished his paper route. "I'm soaked. It's raining cats and dogs out there!"

MEANING: *Raining hard; pouring rain*

ORIGIN: *Some people believe this idiom comes from Norse mythology. In those stories, dogs and cats were associated with wind and storms. But others believe the saying dates back to the 1700s in England. There were many stray dogs and cats in those days. They lived and died in the streets. During massive storms, dead animals and other debris would get swept up in floodwater. This image might make it seem like the animals dropped from the sky during the storm.*

Saved by the bell

Jason and his brother were practicing jumps on their skateboards when Chase, an older neighbor, came by.

"That jump's too small," Chase said. "Why don't you try the one at my house? I bet it's too much for you though. I bet you're too scared."

"No, we're—" Jason started to reply and stopped. Just then he heard his dad calling them in for dinner.

"Whew, that was close!" Jason whispered to his brother as Chase walked away. "Saved by the bell!"

MEANING: *To get out of something you don't want to do because something else comes up; rescued at the last possible moment*

ORIGIN: *This expression comes from the sport of boxing. If a boxer has been knocked to the ground, the referee begins counting to ten. If he gets to ten and the boxer doesn't get up, the match is over. But if the end-of-round bell is rung during the count, they will continue the fight. Both boxers take a short break and then a new round starts. The boxer who was on the ground was "saved" by the bell.*

Smell a rat

Aunt Maria had come to visit. "Mmm," she said, sniffing. "Somebody's been baking cookies!"

"Not us!" said Gloria. "We don't have any cookies, do we?" She elbowed her little sister, who started giggling.

"No!" her sister squeaked, between giggles.

Aunt Maria put her hands on her hips. "I smell a rat!" she said, laughing. "You two are terrible liars. I think you've got some chocolate-chip cookies in here, and I'm going to find them!"

MEANING: *To suspect that someone is not being honest or truthful; to be* ***suspicious***

ORIGIN: *People often associate rats with bad things. Rats are known to spread diseases, too. Cats could easily pick up a rat's scent, so people used cats to keep rats out of their homes. Around the mid-1500s, "smelling a rat" came to mean that you suspected (or "smelled") that something bad or illegal (the "rat") had taken place.*

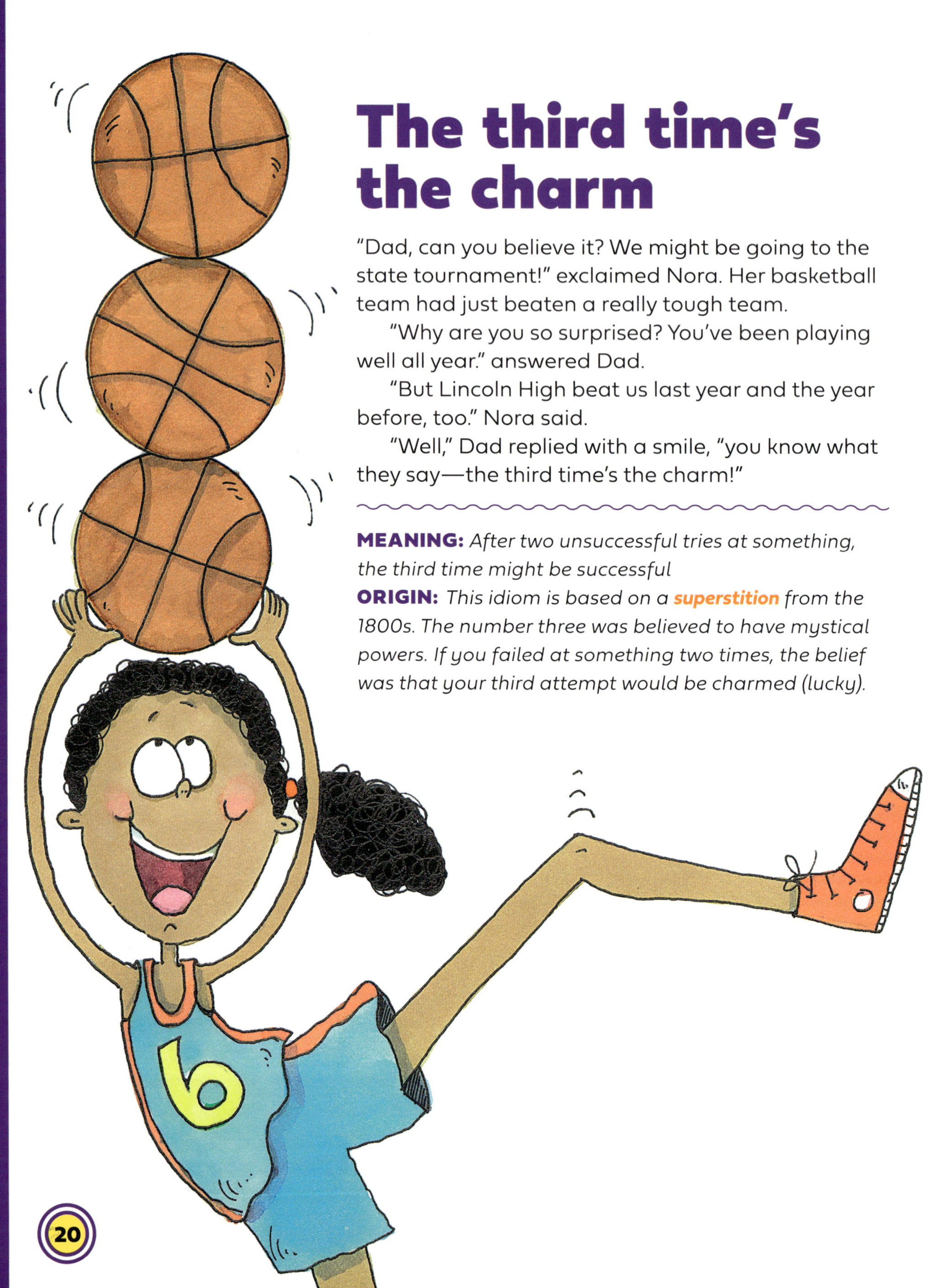

The third time's the charm

"Dad, can you believe it? We might be going to the state tournament!" exclaimed Nora. Her basketball team had just beaten a really tough team.

"Why are you so surprised? You've been playing well all year." answered Dad.

"But Lincoln High beat us last year and the year before, too." Nora said.

"Well," Dad replied with a smile, "you know what they say—the third time's the charm!"

MEANING: *After two unsuccessful tries at something, the third time might be successful*

ORIGIN: *This idiom is based on a* ***superstition*** *from the 1800s. The number three was believed to have mystical powers. If you failed at something two times, the belief was that your third attempt would be charmed (lucky).*

The whole nine yards

Kelsey's big sister was graduating from high school in another month.

"My sister and her friends are really excited," Kelsey told her friend Emmy. "They can't stop talking about it."

"Are they going to do something to celebrate?" asked Emmy.

"They sure are!" Kelsey replied. "They're having a huge party—tons of food, decorations, music, lots of people—the whole nine yards."

MEANING: *Everything*

ORIGIN: *The exact origin of this expression is unknown. The phrase "the whole six yards" was first used in the southern United States around 1912. Over time, the phrase changed from six to nine yards. The meaning of this idiom has always referred to everything you could want or have.*

Glossary

alludes (uh-LOODZ): To talk about or hint at something without mentioning it directly.

deceiving (dih-SEE-ving): To make someone believe something that isn't true; giving a false impression.

euphemism (YOO-fuh-mi-zum): Replacing a word or phrase with another that is less offensive or unpleasant.

expression (ek-SPREH-shun): A common saying; telling or showing your thoughts and feelings.

fable (FAY-bul): A story that is fiction (not true) but helps teach a valuable lesson or share some wisdom.

idioms (ID-ee-umz): Phrases or sayings whose meaning can't be understood by their individual words taken separately.

metaphor (MET-uh-for): Comparing two things by stating that one thing is the other thing.

originated (uh-RIJ-ih-nay-ted): To bring or come into being; to begin.

proverbs (PRAH-vurbz): Popular, often short sayings that express something true and wise.

simile (SIM-uh-lee): A figure of speech comparing two things using *like* or *as*. For example, "shine like a star" is a simile.

slang (SLANG): Informal speech; giving new meanings to old words or inventing new words.

spontaneous (span-TAY-nee-us): Happening freely and naturally, without force; unplanned.

subjective (sub-JEK-tiv): Based on opinions and feelings rather than facts.

superstition (soo-pur-STIH-shun): A belief or practice that isn't grounded in facts; trust in magic or chance.

suspicious (suh-SPIH-shus): To distrust or be distrustful; causing questions or doubt.

Wonder More

- Write a short story using an idiom. You can make up a story or use an experience from your own life. For example, if you choose the idiom "every cloud has a silver lining," you could write about discovering something good in an otherwise bad situation.

- In what ways do idioms impact our writing? In your opinion, do they help improve our ability to tell stories and describe events, or are they unnecessary? Explain your reasoning.

- Think of an idiom that isn't in this book and create a new entry. Write your own brief story using the idiom, and draw a picture to go with it. Then write down its meaning and origin. If you don't know the idiom's origin, where could you learn more about it?

- The idiom "beauty is in the eye of the beholder" from this book means that what one person thinks is beautiful might not be seen as beautiful by someone else. Do you agree or disagree with this idiom's meaning? Describe a time when you saw value or beauty in something, and others disagreed with your viewpoint. Share your story with someone in your class.

Find Out More

In the Library

Heinrichs, Ann. *Similes and Metaphors.* Mankato, MN: The Child's World, 2020.

Pearson, Yvonne, and Mernie Gallagher-Cole (illustrator). *Rev Up Your Writing in Fictional Stories.* Mankato, MN: The Child's World, 2016.

Schubert, Susan, and Raquel Bonita (illustrator). *I'll Believe You When . . . Unbelievable Idioms from around the World.* Minneapolis, MN: Lerner, 2020.

Zafarris, Jess. *Once Upon a Word: A Word-Origin Dictionary for Kids.* Emeryville, CA: Rockridge Press, 2020.

On the Web

Visit our website for links about idioms: **childsworld.com/links**

Note to Parents, Caregivers, Teachers, and Librarians: We routinely verify our Web links to make sure they are safe and active sites. So encourage your readers to check them out!

Index